TO: ______________________________

FROM: ______________________________

Published by Sellers Publishing, Inc.
161 John Roberts Road, South Portland, ME 04106
Visit us at www.sellerspublishing.com • E-mail: rsp@rsvp.com

 Like Us on Facebook

ISBN-13: 978-1-4162-4531-5

Printed and bound in China.

10 9 8 7 6 5 4 3 2 1

LOVE YOU TO THE MOON AND BACK

LOVE DOESN'T MAKE THE WORLD GO 'ROUND, LOVE IS WHAT MAKES THE RIDE WORTHWHILE

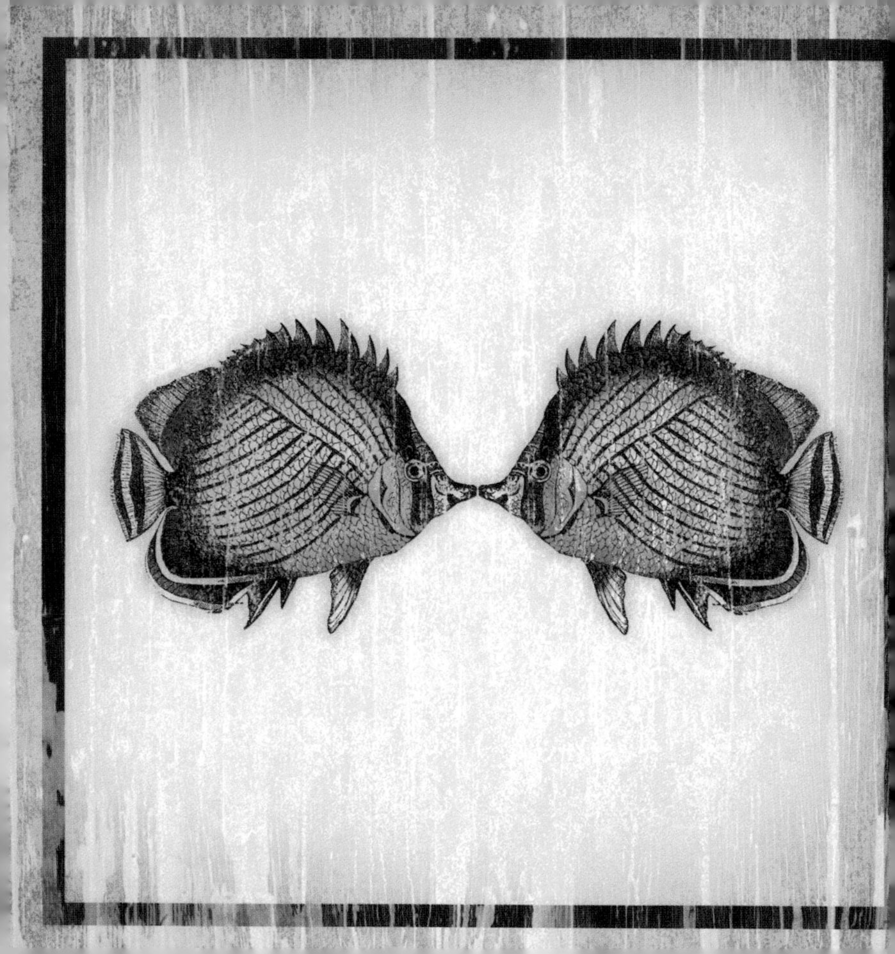

OF ALL OF THE FISH
IN THE SEA
I CHOSE YOU AND
YOU CHOSE ME

YOU MAKE ME

HAPPY

WHEN SKIES ARE GRAY

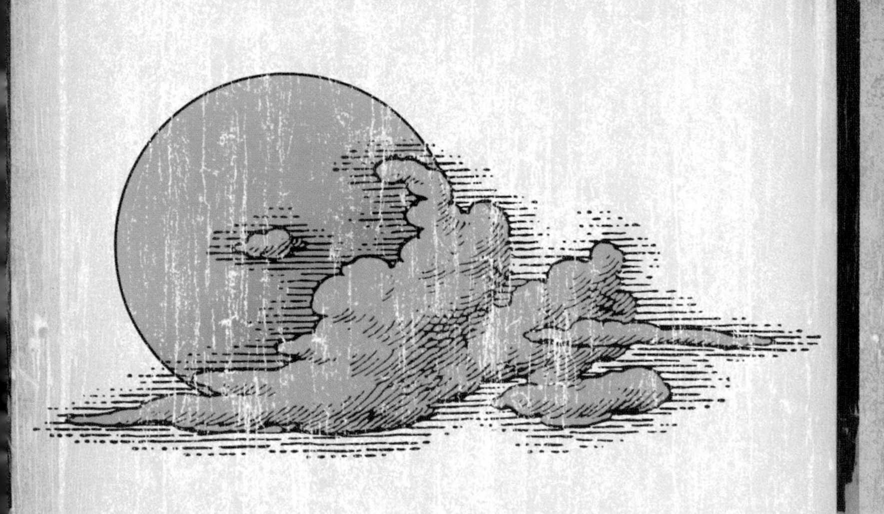

I LOVE YOU
MORE THAN
CUPCAKES

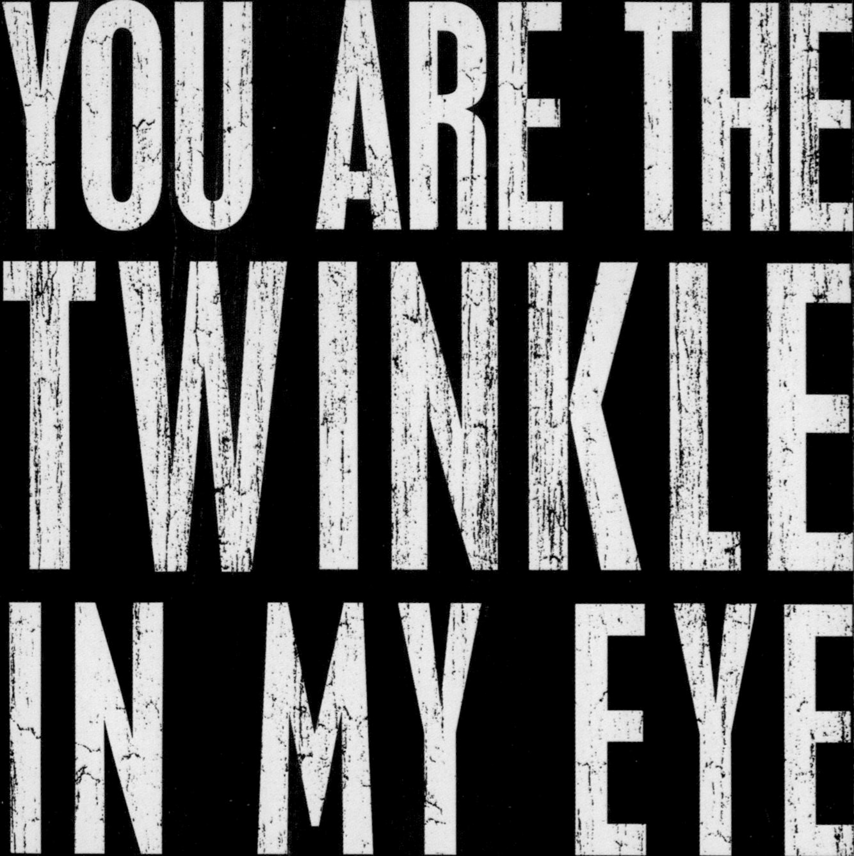
YOU ARE THE
TWINKLE
IN MY EYE

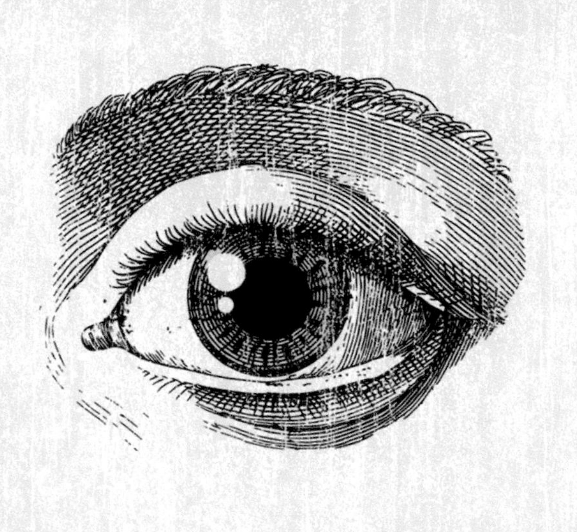

MADE BY NEW HAVEN CLOCK CO NEW HAVEN

YOU'RE EVERY
MINUTE OF
MY EVERYDAY

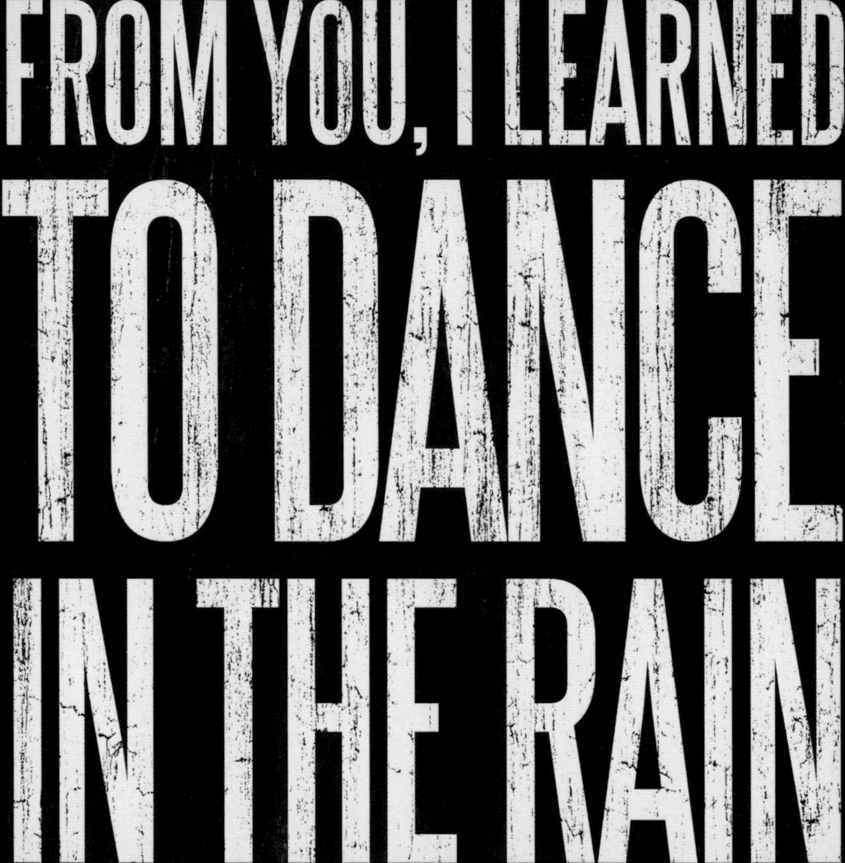
FROM YOU, I LEARNED
TO DANCE
IN THE RAIN

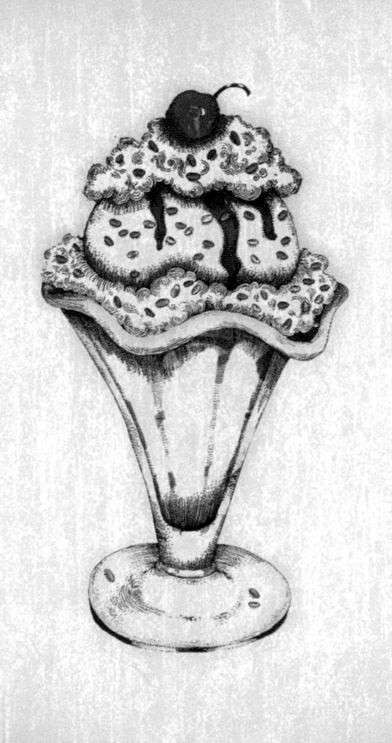

YOU ARE THE
CHERRY ON
MY SUNDAE

THE MOST WONDERFUL THING I CHOSE TO DO WAS SHARE MY LIFE AND HEART WITH YOU

EVERY LOVE STORY
IS BEAUTIFUL
BUT OURS IS MY
FAVORITE

LOVE YOU TO
THE MOON
AND BACK

MILK

YOU ARE THE MILK TO MY COOKIES

YOU ARE THE
PEANUT BUTTER
TO MY JELLY

YOU ARE THE

BLUE

IN MY SKY

YOU ARE MY
FOREVER
AND ALWAYS

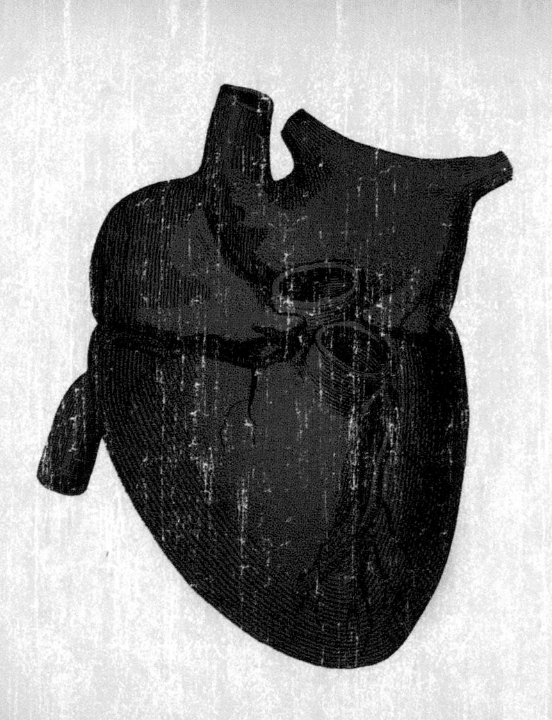

I PLEDGE ALL
MY LOVE
ALL MY LIFE

I'LL NEVER MISS AN
OPPORTUNITY
TO TELL YOU
I LOVE YOU

Love

LOVE IS
SWEET

YOU KNOW YOU'RE IN LOVE
WHEN YOU CAN'T FALL ASLEEP
BECAUSE REALITY IS FINALLY
BETTER THAN
YOUR DREAMS

YOU MAKE
MY HEART
SMILE

I CAN'T SAY
I LOVE YOU ENOUGH
SO THIS IS A REMINDER

I Love You

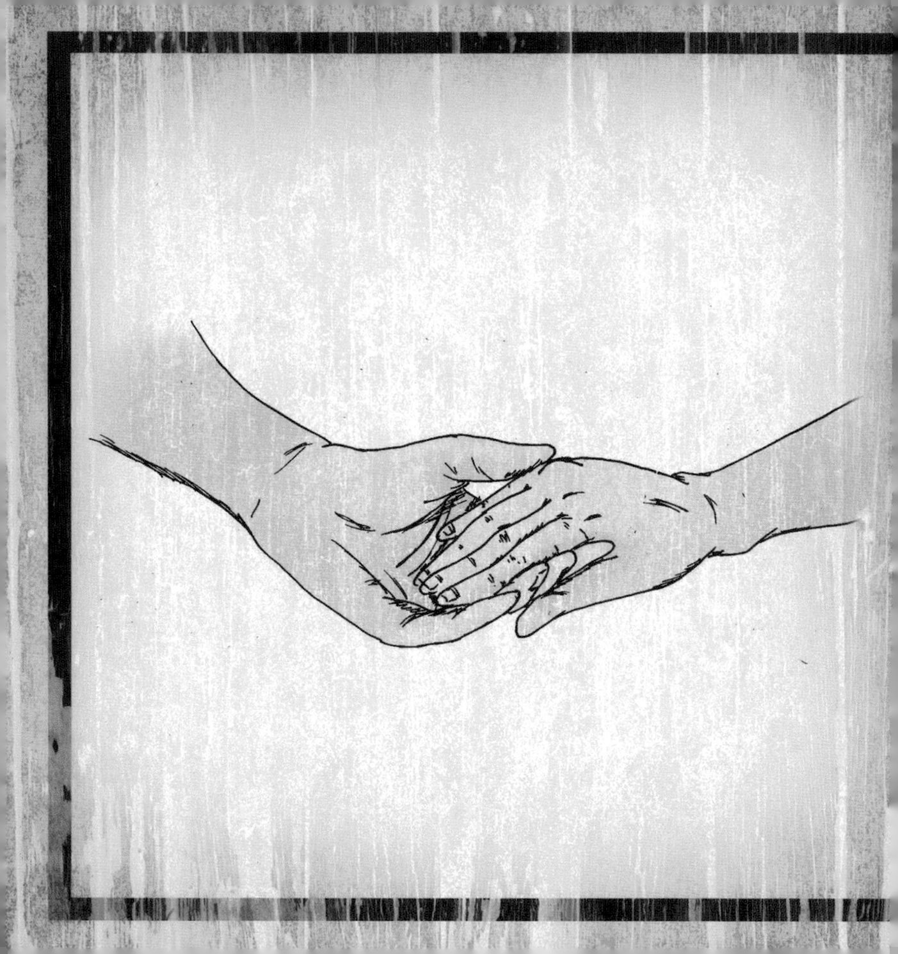

LET'S LOVE FOREVER AND A DAY

YOU ARE THE

MAC

AND THE CHEESE

YOU ARE THE

WATER

TO MY OCEAN

YOU ARE THE

LACES

TO MY SHOES

LIFE BRINGS US
TO UNEXPECTED PLACES
BUT LOVE BRINGS US
HOME

WITH LOVE
THERE ARE ALWAYS
MIRACLES

OUR LOVE
IS SWEET

YOU ARE MY SUNSHINE

ALWAYS KISS ME
GOOD NIGHT
ALWAYS KISS ME
GOOD MORNING